AF263710

ISBN 978-0-392-09944-5

RED

by
Elizabeth Faria

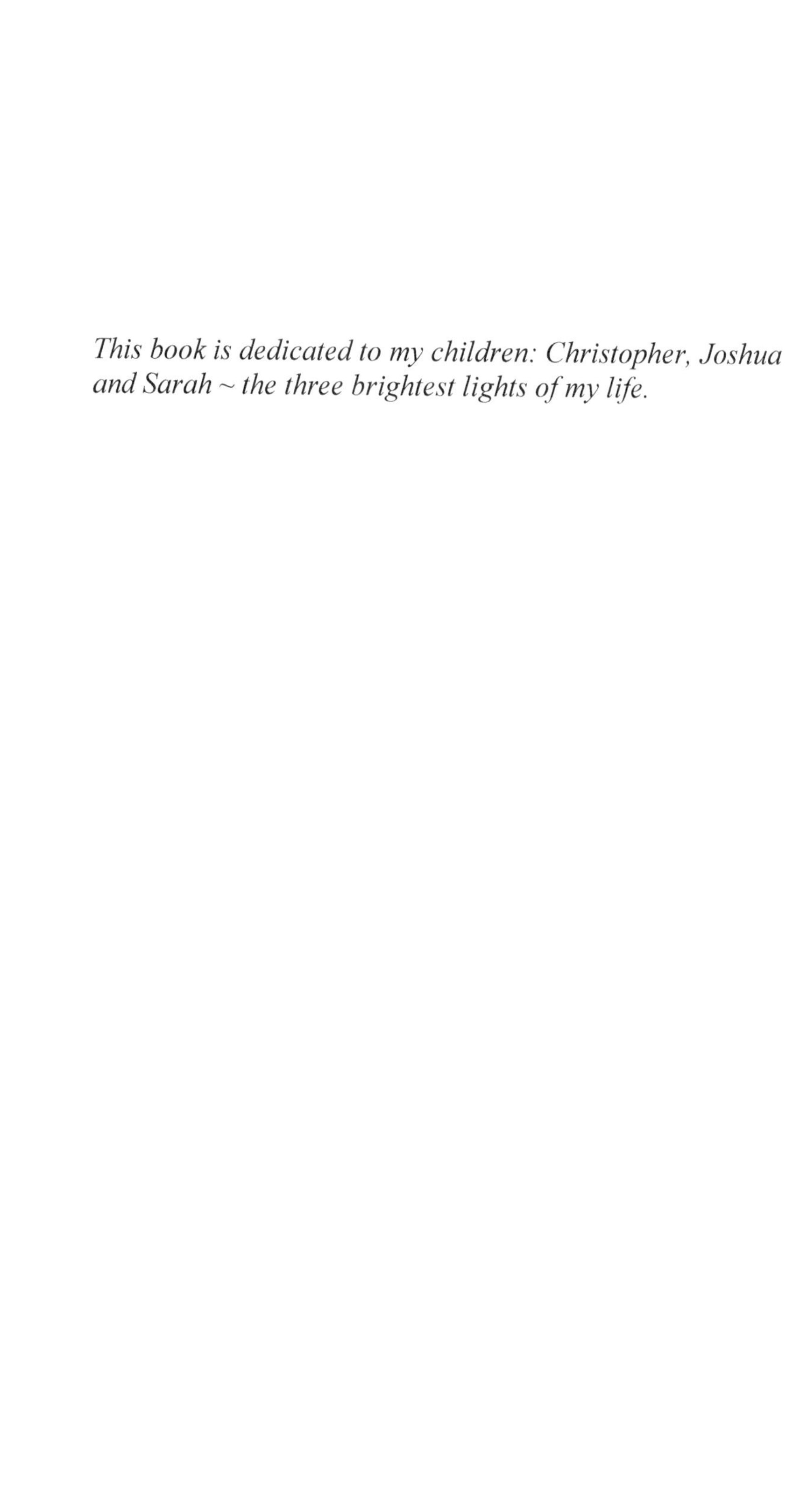

This book is dedicated to my children: Christopher, Joshua and Sarah ~ the three brightest lights of my life.

A collection of over 25 years of creative expression.
The terrain of this journey is varied and includes such
forms as sonnets, haiku, villanelles, ballads, triolets, free
verse, narrative, nonsense, and others which meander
through the beautiful pathways of Poetry: Using Ordinary
Words in Extraordinary Ways.

There's rough and smooth. Dark and light. Up and down.
Progress and regression. Pain and pleasure. Joy and
misery. Love and loss. And isn't that the journey of us all?

CONTENTS

RED

THE MATCH

I await, dormant
In a dark box
Cold, unignited
A torment
Of potential
Lying in sequential
Rows of counted sticks
A ripping wish
To be extracted
And lighted,
Yet a fear
Of the sear,
The burst-blast brighted
Meteor match
Raging incineration rushing
Cardboard consumed
In a brilliant bloom
Then, boom!
A dying breath
Too soon
Extinguishes the ecstasy
Fueled in a painful flash
Agony across the abrasive
Required pass.
However, I am treated
In an unheated
Handling–
Choose, choose me!
I would be
A conduit for candling.

Transfer of a combustive cause
Risen from casket
To creation
Rough-raked raw
Then red revelation
The exquisite explosion
Not trimmed or dimmed
But relayed in a matched motion
Feeding the fuse,
Wonderful connecting to wire
Passion passed
And thus reuse
My fire.

THE WELL

"Talk to me!"
You prod,
Forcefully fingering
My fragile emotions.
"Tell me what's wrong,
What's bothering you."
I clam up
Shut my shell
And throw me down
A deep well,
I cannot stand
To have my
Bucket brought up.
"I'm listening,"
You insist.
So I come up
Just a little.
It starts to feel good–
I come up
Just a little more.
Then stop,
Jolted abruptly–
Interruptedly
You say
All you can
About you–
It's true,
You do it every time.
I listen

Still, aware
Watching, waiting
For a moment
That is mine
But your voice
Goes on and on
A constant flow–
And yet you
Want to know
What I hide.
So I go
Deep inside–
I bring my bucket
All the way up–
You take your cup
To fill it full
But I am empty,
As usual.

WHICH ONE

You know they say timing is everything
And the world rotates in such a pattern
In the morning the gifted trill birds sing
At night the sun on the horizon burns
A moment sooner, a moment later
One step here, one step there–what would be missed?
To take the stairs or the elevator?
Choice A or Choice B–is there fate in this?
If I'd not met you, I'd meet some other?
Can one be right or is it just the clock?
How can the earth hold two many lovers?
Double count of ships and only one dock?
I do not know which step has made this match
But fear I must find content with the catch.

SURFACE

Snagged
Ragged trip
A rosy rip
In unaffected flesh
Small, unpainful
No nerves sending notes
To rally the brain and heart
For an injury's cause
A nick only noticeable
By sight.
I am hurt,
And I have been hurt
By you
But the surface is
Merely skin scratched.
When you inflict me
I cannot feel pain
So–see a lash
The crimson greedy gash
It activates the red
But I do not ache
Like I once did
For more than flesh is dead.

BOILING POINT

I lay
and I yearn
And burn
Inside
Longing
For your touch
I need it so much...

Do you notice?
Do you even care?
That I am there
Full of wanting
And nothing,
Nothing is mine...

I hope with time,
Maybe time
Can make you feel
A deeper feel
For me, for us
And then you'll long too
For a touch
Of much
Love
And mutual need
And feed
My painful starving
Till there's no more hunger inside...

Now here I lay
And it's day
But deep within it's night
Because you're beside me
And I feel as close as
I am the boiling core
And you are the crust and
I need so much more...

I lay so awake
With an ear
Of fear
That penetrates deep
Because I hear you
As I listen to your
Very, very
Sound sleep.

BALLAD OF SWEET SUSAN

Sweet Susan cared too much for love
To wrap like a blanket around her
Or wear on her hand as a glove
Enshrouds the wearer to make warmer.

Sweet Susan sought for a sweet cover
Down dark in a deep black pit
But was buried by a cold lover
Who had never a fire lit.

Yet hoping for a source to make bright
Sweet weak Susan hopefully stayed
Though the blanket was cold and light
Love makes hope brave and not afraid.

Till soon Sweet Susan all a-shiver
Cooled down to a lesser degree,
Gave it all as a naive giver
Living cold but comfortably.

Temperate to the temperature
Blackly acquired a shallower need–
Sweet Susan once so warm and pure
Had not a fire nor spark to feed.

Not a glove or scarf or hat,
A coat–one surely would not fit
Who used to care too much for that
Now did not care a whit.

She had a blanket; it was enough
Though pastly she quivered under
The lack of feeling and fluff
But somehow now it warmed her.

YOUR HANDS HAVE NO AFFECTION

Your hands have no affection
Surely blood throughout body circulates
But not reaching the ends of your arms
They are always cold and I hate
Their death without resurrection
The chill that never warms

I have waited for their flowing
I have longed for any moment of heat
But the pulsing stops at your wrists
The track around is incomplete
The racing in reckless going
Bloodless filtering of your fists

I have felt and seen in other men
The lifeness of their fingers
Leaving burns from the trailing tips
As any burn does linger
Raking remembrance of their skin
Hot-scarring fossils of their grip

I carry across me these marks
Made by hands that are not yours
I feel the soreness of their touch
And the pain that there's not more
I wear them warmly in the dark
I am silent, but they speak much

And in their scorching chatter
Wordful wounds reminding me
Of the fiery fingers burning
Blaze stroking, stoking of my body
Fueling past passionate matter
Coals made brighter with the turning

Oh! How they call in their faded flesh!
Beating beneath the strikes unseen
And your hands frosty, polar pawing
Incapable crossing of the screen
Solid separation of mesh
Present and past: freezing, thawing

In your hands I turn to timber
Felled and forgotten till your need
But sparking in my surface and soul
Is a better, brighter seed
Flickering flint forgets, remembers–
I'm in halfness, but once was whole.

MOURNERS

A drought is happiness. I've learned the flood
Comes as torrent tears from eyes, from sad skies,
Crop killing in waist-high wet, murk and mud,
Sobbing for cycles in which good seed dies.
The water washes down; blanketing grief
Covers everything of heart, land and leaf
And we would wish to sand it up and save
Our harvest but instead must give to grave.
Man cannot curve Nature, curb time away–
Make loves last or the heavens shut and stay;
Or I would gladly live in the desert
Cottoned from seasons share of passing pain
Sheltered in excluded expanse from hurt,
Dry to death and no ravishes of rain.

I CAME TO YOU

I came to you
Cleaned
All my glory
Gleaned
Into one
Proud presentation
So carefully
All my colors
Applied
Glamour glossed
Into a
Perfect, beautiful
Me
Every effort just
For you
To see
This appearance
Extraordinary
Fantastic fashioning
Of divine dust
I waited for
A rainbow
Of approval
Like a volcanic bust
But, honey,
All you
Handed me
Was rust.

BIRD AND MAN

There is a bird upon the tree–
Speaks not a word, just looks at me
Holding in his beak a fresh worm
Declares it dead! It cannot be!

And in my self I start to squirm
Reminding me my head is firm
He did not say, "I caught to kill"
Yet stated such, in eyes, his term.

The worm lay dead upon the hill
Thrown from his mouth, the shriekest trill
His catch is cold and fully whole,
Away he flies, what need to fill.

Man in nature, a cros'sed hole
A heart as empty as a bowl
To act without a bit of soul,
To act without a bit of soul.

STONE

You are a weight
You taint
Everything you touch
Drag it down so much
Your mental madness
Superficial sadness
All funnel
To a singular tunnel:
You.
Tornadic tumult
Carving craziness
It's what you do.
Twisting truth
Bending gray
Till you think it's right
Yet black and white
For everyone else.
Inflated sense of self
You manipulate with ease
Perfected brain disease
You leave behind leftovers
Scraps of lives
That you shred
As you charge ahead
Stepping on trails of
Tattered hearts
Caring none
About the parts.

SPLINTER

He is doing it again
That which I hate
He knows I'm angry
And wants me to explain
But it is useless, vain
And I push it down deep
To join all the others
They have been there so long
From the beginning
I have resigned myself
That there is no winning
This battle
Every feeling I have is infectious
Without any hope of festering to expulsion
Instead they are kept in muted revulsion
Never to surface.

My obliviously trailing fingers
Forced the wood to splinter me
I did not notice the tiny fleck
Until days later–
And when I tried to pluck it free
The skin had grown over,
It became part of me.

SOMEONE ELSE'S LIGHT

Someone else's light
Is illuminating my porch
Someone else's hand
Is carrying my torch
I had a light that hung
Above the railing and cement
But it burned out and darkness
Was all I seemed to get
And I had a torch that flamed
In my hand, all big and bright
But the blaze belly emptied
And my arm grew frail and light
And I stood in my house
Where the bulbs barely glowed
All torchless and porchless
But I guess it never showed.

SECTIONS

In a sudden, cruel separation
That tore apart my soft-chambered heart
I sought hope of resuscitation
That the full beating might newly start
Hollow portion, drained of living
Sad emptiness could not be filled
And I hurt for the want of giving
Yet my soul's reserves were freely sealed
I felt an affected organ's part
The one deep-changed section of the four
Was dying within my heart,
I quietly shut that chamber door
And painfully the sacrificed piece
Severed; I built a fresh partition
Since the fourth fragment had lost its lease
Forcing a permanent division
The remaining three began to pound
Continuing on only a third–
Surprisingly, endurance was found
And the makeshift muscle wakened, whirred
As strength was fashioned within its core
Though the martyred part is ever gone–
Thus, living on less it lives on more
For willed by me, my heart must beat on.

CONQUER

Drown me in my cares
My sorrows, my woes
Abandon me to foes
And those
That hate me.
Grate me
Up and down
Leave me
Surrounded
By a million
Legions of stress.
Undress
My dignity–
My person
Naked and exposed.
Take all that you can
From me and
What do you suppose
Will be left?
A person better than before
And not a whit bereft!

DEATH LEAVES A ROTTING FORM

Death leaves a rotting form but nurtured love lives on
Refusing to decompose in crumb-tossed black earth,
To find an empty host; farewell, the weak one's gone.
First grew the feeling slow as the start of a yawn
Stretched pity to wrap the heart of transient birth
Death leaves a rotting form, but nurtured love lives on.
Gentle roots bud forth in the tender-soiled lawn
Abiding till uprooted from the land-locked serf
To find an empty host; farewell, the weak one's gone.
Heart, confident of vict'ry, displayed beating brawn
But doomed it celebrated with ill-fated mirth;
Death leaves a rotting form, but nurtured love lives on.
An infirm heart shriveled, grew increasingly wan
Love, heedless, expanded its emotional girth
To find an empty host; farewell, the weak one's gone.

BENDING

I must be flexible
Or I will break
Adversity is not fair
Shows no care
As to who it will snap.
I cannot have a
Fragile spine–
Be full of sap
Like the pine.

The oak
It tries
But being rooted
Is unbending
And unwise.

But–see the birch
Slender and tender
In the storm and wind,
Arches it back but
Also bows its head.
I, too, must so bend.

THE BALLAD OF LILY MAE

It was cold and gray and Lily Mae
Knew the sun was setting fast
Yet she took a path that cold, gray day
Which woefully could be her last.

Though the trail lay dark and rough and wet
It was the end that held her prize,
And that's what made Lily Mae forget
With sunshine bright in her eyes.

A quick little jaunt, then on her way
Down the lane that led to Eric Cloud
Her heart turned her girlfeet astray
While the thunder threatened loud.

It was supper soon, she knew too well
And mama's fierceness would get gray
If the ringing of the dinner bell
Did not produce Lily Mae.

She quickened her beat and made her feet
Skip faster to get a quick look
No time for her mother's flaming heat
To flame out the detour she took.

A beating's worth a glance of him
A glance that'll cover the night
With dreams of a boy tall and slim
And blue eyes with frosty sight.

Just the thought of his eyes, cool and blue
Gave warmth to our dear Lily Mae
And his hair as black as the sky that flew
Into a rage on that cold, gray day.

Rain began to sprinkle a warning:
This is not your path, Lily Mae!
Forget this road of heartache and mourning
Don't tempt this cold, gray day!

But Lily Mae could not hear
The cry of the wise sky above
Could only see blue eyes dear
The look of her frosty love.

A love that gave fearless flight
To her poor little fearful feet
That were now black with a muddy night,
'Tis love which shoved her down that street.

A love that made her soaking clothes
Of no consequence to her goal
For she simply could not feel her woes
When Eric burned warm in her soul.

Oh! That beautiful Eric Cloud!
So very handsome and charming was he–
And the thunder bellowed deafening loud
With the waves of the sky like the sea.

The rain that dropped like big, wet eggs
That pelted the path away
And poor Lily Mae's little legs
Were growing cold and gray.

Faster, she thought, faster still!
But with each step the rain matched her pace
And the ditches like bowls, began to fill
While the rain masked Lily's face.

I'll get there yet, I will, I will!
Lily screamed as she struggled so,
But the fury of the sky was shocking shrill
For it knew what she did not know.

Keep her away! The lightning vowed
And she'll never know the gray day
That will come when charming Eric Cloud
Coldly throws our poor Lily away.

For handsome he was, 'tis very true
A smile that seemed like the sun
And eyes filled with a chill of blue
And not a love for anyone.

Yes, he'd be fast her heart to take
Never one to turn adoration away
Then shortly he'd cause a painful break
And toss our sweet Lily away.

For a heart as pure as Lily Mae's
Is only found in the content of rain
But Eric's soul was cold and gray
And only delivered pain.

And Lily thought that she knew pain–
Her mama was fierce and hot,
But the storm and the rain
Knew of pain that sweet Lily did not.

The switch of a stick would hold no heat
It would seem like zero degrees
Compared to her heart when it did not beat
When cold Eric caused it to freeze.

Keep her away! Keep her away!
The rain it raged in defense!
Harder, harder on Lily Mae
Gush toward the crooked fence!

And the ditches rose to meet the road
The side currents rushing on
The thunder screamed in its murderous throat
Be strong! Be strong! Be strong!

Lily Mae was faltering even though
She fought like a wild, wet buck
Just a few more steps to the end of the road
She would make it there with luck.

But luck was not on her side that day
She fell hard in the deep, muddy street
The night beyond cold and gray–
'Twas the sky swept Lily off her feet.

She clawed the ground that sucked her down
Down toward the churning ditch
With the water swirling round and round
Like the cauldron of a witch.

Though Lily fought she could not beat
The fate of the sentencing rain
That drowned her down for taking that street
That kept her from knowing true pain.

The sky cheered black and bloodless, Lily Mae
You never saw your Eric Cloud
Down you went on that cold, gray day
Down to the highest cloud.

Up to the sunshine your sweet heart fell
Now happy in heart, hand and soul
While your mama rings her dinner bell
Getting madder with each toll.

WEEDS

The boy was man
He began
As a short
Small seed
Slap him hard
Make him a
Tough breed
No tears
Can't cry
Work hard all day
For a man's pay
Put bread on the table
And earn!
Learn
About life
Have a wife
And a couple of kids
Especially sons
Tough ones
Like you
Continue on
Pass the genes
The boiled-dry stew
Till there's no more boys
Just strong men
Big tall weeds
That are tough as
Wild grown
But carefully sown
Seeds.

PLAYING BALL

Hard to decide
Who's the loser,
The chosen or
The chooser.
Neither side
Can hope for winning
A single inning
When the teams
From the beginning
Were so mismatched.
Throw a ball
They cannot catch it
Whether outfielder
Or in it.
Never a call
At the bases
So untouched
No sliding
Even slight to tell
But heaped higher and higher–
Neglect is a busy builder
No common crier,
"Safe!" to yell–
Can't even gain a first.
The players' constant thirst
In the dugout hot and low
Has drunk the cooler empty
And there's no more.
It's an embarrassing score:

Zero to Zero.
Once there was
But now aren't any
Fans cheering seated–
The crowd grew old and tired
And retreated.
But still the team plays ball
Though never scoring
Or even placing
On the field–
No balls over the wall,
Only pacing
And that is all.

THE BEE

The bee
When landing on fear
On destiny
On fateful falling
Instinctively
Injects the bite
To produce the painful
Swollen protrusion,
Instantly inflamed intrusion
And save itself from
The harm and hurt
But fly away
Only
To die.

In meeting one who
Measures out extraction
I landed foolishly
Without the speed
Of retraction
Disarmed obliviously
And left to die
Without even a
Dose of defense,
Stinger removed
As the bee.

BATTLE

I watch you
Turn in circles
Like a cat
To find the perfect position
Behind your ever-present barracks.
I sigh–
I am used to these attacks
That pounce on me, then
Playfully paw my emotions
Before the kill–
But this time I will
Not be numbered
Among the dead–
I head
Off vulnerability
With the coldest chill
And jump behind
My personal mound
With ricocheting ground
Heaped high.
I am prepared
Against your petty warfare
So let the arrows fly.

COATED

Men cannot endure.
Women shaking seasonless
Without fur
Less and left
And bereft–
Brrrr!
Oh, we have been
So very, very cold
With nothing to hold
But ourselves.
We have gathered and garnered
Every pelt
But never felt
The insulation
Just skinned and sewed
And gave away
Our identification
The connected coat
Warming the throat
Of a man.
When we are older
We can
Remove our work
Thinking it cannot be hard
To be hardy
In the winter,
We have been
Womanly bare
For years

Not even a flake
Of acclimation
Just shake and shift
And shiver
In mute modification.
So coatless is he
And freezing
Sudden shocking thermostat
He cannot endure
Where he is at
Though we have been here
For timeless turnovers
There is no pity in
This animal–
And he leaves,
Unable to climate adjust.
Where is fairness?
She asks,
She demands!
She must.

THE RUG

Did you see
What came out
His head?
First was bleeding,
Now is dead
Leaving a cemented circle
Of a hard and crusted red.
We have carried
His body
Long away
Laid him down
In just one day
Covered corpse in
The required ways–
But here the
Crimson circumference
Stays.
She is dizzy as a drug
From where over and over
She did scrub
The stained fibers
Of the rug
Upon her knees–
But everyday she sees
A sick shadow
On the square
And death outpouring
Brings back mourning
And keeps it there.

She bought soap
She bought brush
In a frenzied cleaning rush
Scraped the wool
Upon the floor
A thousand times
A carpet cleaning crush
Of a bubbled hope
To clean and clear
The scarlet spot it bore–
But he cried with every pass
As he lay beneath the grass
That had been forgotten
And it showed
In the towering daisies unmowed
And now as graved
Deeply dungeoned
From the blow that bludgeoned
When he fell hard
On the Oriental score
The running red
Falling, falling
From his head
As the falling fluid
Disturbed the pattern
On the floor.
Though he hast no power
To shorten even
A single flower
He has willed
The thickly substance

Down into the fiber
Deeply to remind her
Of the blow that blew
Him far away
Of the man that came in anger
That day
Busting broken through the door
Wielding whack upon
The living till
The living lived no more.
And she came and found
Him on the floor–
Crying, screaming
As she
Gathered up the broken
While his head streaming
Flowed free a token
Though no words of course
Were spoken
He left it there.
She could not bear
To see it every day
But over and over it did prove
Resistant to remove
And the boards too cold without it
So it stayed.
She has ceased her
Useless scrubbing
And the redness like ink
Has faded through the years
Of feet over fiber rubbing

It to a soft pink.
But still it remains.
She has ceased to visit
His stone
Unchanged
in the garden,
All alone
And the grass so tall and fielding
A daisy harvest it is yielding
And he would harrow in his hollow
At the thought
That her feet no longer follow
With tears and sobbing,
Wailing
Wallow
But finds him smiling in his grot
Knowing his stain
Though somewhat failing
Is embedded in the rug
So he lies assured and smug
At her pain–
Rosy remembrance
Insistent on the floor
That she recalls him
Lying there instead
Forevermore.

BANKING

How can you expect
Our account to amount
To anything
When you have
Invested
Nothing?
I know you
Think you've made
Some decent deposits
And you
Expect to
Receive dividends
From these
Delusions
And you
Want my
Interest
To grow–
But it cannot–
Long ago
Due to neglect and
Poor management of funds
Our account
Stopped being joint
And I
Permanently
Withdrew.

WHITENED

Let loose the black past
Feel it fall–it's forgotten
Cover me with white.

COMPOST

Patch up your pain. It is compost
Compiled of year and tears, most
Rancid and rich and ready to
Fertilize a new, hungry host–

You've compacted your best, you know,
Rejected rinds, leftover stew,
Broken seals and expired dates–
Yet you've recycled; wise to do.

So many pass it through the grates
Scraped clean from hasty, childish plates
But you have layered old loves down
Extending them beyond the gates

To feed new growth in the ground
The circle continues around–
Better yield and nourishment found,
Better yield and nourishment found.

THE EMERGENCY VOLUNTEER

She was paid to work with type, paper, pen
And show up at ten. She knows how to file,
Answer the phone, smile, be there promptly when
They need a good clerk. She's been there a while.
But this job is new, and conditions vile.
How could've she complained, sitting at her desk?
No dresses blood-stained to bring up her bile–
She is so untrained, as all of the rest
Of the women here, who bandage up men
Dying and shot through. But she must learn fast
Or they will drop here as on field again–
Oh what war will do with each heinous blast!
To break the clear glass of each windowed view
And see not in white, but in red and blue.

THE FAN

She sits flirting feignly with her fan
She knows she can
Whisk fabric in waves
Held in hand
And like an encouraging bellow
Pump the heart of some poor fellow.
With lowered lashes flitter
Hummingbird eyes that pitter
In the wooing refined graces
Fluttering rows of windowed laces
Across the room–
Later, he'll be pushed as with broom
Swept dusty in her pan
Another fallen to the floor
From the fluency of her fan.
But now she eyes
The one too shy
To even sign her card
The target desirable and dumb
Oh, how easily they come
And their fall the all more hard.
He meets her eyes–
Quick, the showy shield is placed
She can hear his beating race
See the blushing of his face
Without disguise
Triumphant laughter behind
Her barricade.
He is slowly advancing
To ask her for the dancing

A parade of practiced prancing
On the stage.
She has him now in cage
And thus is done, as the song
When the newly notes are ceasing
She is much past pleasing
Her silken gown creasing
And is gone.
He rattles in a rage
Ne'er so blatantly abused
Casually, callously used
Continuance refused
What wicked sporting smiling
Heartless hunting and beguiling
She is blinking at another bloke as blind
And forced her fan within his mind
Now breathless from the racing
The abandonment of pacing
Swirling chandeliers in ceiling
Bowing low before her, reeling
He practically worships in his kneeling–
She accepts.
She conquers each without regret
Trophy-mounted
Hardly counted
Since she began
To shoot hearts of miserable men
O'er and o'er again
Because she can
Not with gun
But with her fan.

FLOWERS FOR SARAH

She was conceived as a seed-planted rose.
Nine-month nourishment: soil, water; sows
The birth of precious green unseen then grows
Sprouting, shouting leaf, laugh, petal and prose–
Oh sweetness! The beauty of bud which flows
Lovely from grass to girl in curl and clothes.
She arose from earth, from me–how she glows
In opening–Glorious!–I suppose
I should be glad. But sad how clipped time blows
Buds away, the cradled babe, toddler toes–
Now fully brimmed and bloomed (too soon!) she goes
Fast in flowering. Only Mother knows
The ache to relive and watch her young Rose.

I. SHE IS GOING TO GIVE HIM AWAY

Clamp
The cord,
Severed and shut.
Her last tie
to this little life.
She could not be wife,
or even girlfriend
She was just receiver,
But now will be giver.
They are waiting,
So anxiously, happy
For him
To take away too soon
From this room
that she has memorized.
He cries.
Does she want to see him?
See his eyes?
Or forget?
Forget the nine months,
His tiny kicks.
Their joy at each ultrasound,
Her mounting misery.
He.
He has no name.
They will name him.
She has no claim
To Baby Boy.
The pain and pressure
relieved at delivery

But never past.
They took him away,
Way too fast–
For his first bath.
When he is clean,
He will be in
Their arms
And she will never
See the soft blue hat
Upon his head.
She will fill in her breasts
That will wonder
Where he is to suck
Away the pain–
The unbearable pain
In her chest.

II. SHE TAKES HIM BACK

They painted pale blue
The room which used
To be an office.
They gladly bought crib,
Bumper, stroller, new car seat
Instead of new car
Or new vacation.
But lots of new clothes–
Lots of tiny blue ones.
They had a baby shower–
They received presents
Rattles and bibs and

Burp cloths and pacifiers and
All things baby boy.
Oh! What they have invested!
And so sure–everyone was
So, so sure.
They unpacked and unpackaged
And threw away receipts
And envisioned kissing small fingers
and small feet.
But were unprepared
for unexpectedness.
They never even laid
Him down on the bed for one night
Their right
Was ripped
In a dizzying decision,
A rent revision
Years of waiting wishful
For one to give what
They cannot have–
They loved him from
the very first yes.
And now a
No.
Where will it go–
The ready room,
The mobile still,
Quiet as all the rest
Except for the running,
Unbearable pain
In their chests.

HE IS GOING OFF TO WAR

He is going off to war at nineteen
My nephew born in nineteen-eighty-six
Oldest son of my oldest brother, Rick.
Why'd he have to join the Army? He's green.
His young girlfriend has a silver dog tag
Around her neck–she got it at the mall,
As if she has claim to his name at all.
His buddies joined him; all signed up to brag,
To fight, defend, with shortest hair and crawl
Again like they did long ago. Please find
Another aunt, not as kind, who won't mind
Or whose memories don't freshly recall
Pushing him hard in the swing at the park–
"Faster! Higher! Go, go, go!" Don't go, Mark.

STORIES

Your profile is outlined against
The flaky, scaly wall
And I think your eyes are green
Behind the gray shadow of
Oversized sunglasses.
I sit enraptured at the base
Of your thick feet and listen
To your stories...
"We were very rich in Russia–
Owned streets of fancy department stores.
When we fled we swallowed diamonds,
The only way we could carry anything
Across the line."
She pauses to cover a phlegmy cough.
"It was not a good time to be a Jew."
She reaches under a plastic frame to wipe
Spontaneously watering eyes.
"I went to China for refuge and had a maid
with bound feet. She took off her wraps once
and I cried when I saw her twisted toes.
They scared me!"
My grandma and I laugh together as
She hands me a hot piroshki.
"Then we came here. But we
were never all together again.
One of us was here, one there."
I sit on the expanse of her lived-in lap,
adding weight to the miles of her legs
That walked from Russia
To China, to me.

THE LITTLE DRUMMER BOY

He is young
He has a drum
Which hangs suspended from his neck
Like a musical noose.
He is marching
Amongst the arching
Of artillery
The loud, loose
Cannons and musky muskets
Bodies filling and falling
Into ditches like buckets
Brimmed with the dead
He must not lose his head
His fingers shaking
Hands must be forced into making
The proper beat.
He who is told he is brave
But secretly, shamefully
Dreams of retreat.
His feet
Falter, walking hell–
Samuel, the one he played cards with,
Just fell
At the front
Of the bloodied line
He is behind,
A back-row seat,
Forced to view the red
Which later, if he sleeps

Will revisit him in bed.
The wooden sticks weigh
Heinous and heavy
To such thin, new arms.
He thinks of home
Of Johnny,
Of the farm.
He misses his brother
And cries for his mother
When no one sees him
In uniform.
1, 1-2-3, 1, 1-2-3
It is not melody,
Certainly not harmony–
He does not know what it is for.
He has never dared
To demonstrate a tear.
He swallows fear.
He is scared
He is young
He was not prepared
For war
Or for this drum.

TRIUMPHANT JEW AT AUSCHWITZ

Here I am
In a camp
Wrenched from
The life I knew
Things taken
That I did
Not give
And made
To live in a hell.
I've suffered well
My tortures
My ceaseless nights
Of dark laments
I've prayed to God
With waterless lips
And eyes that
Could not spare
One more tear
For childless hips.
I've swallowed
Food laden with the
Filthiest rot
My fingers shaking
In a feathered prayer
Over a weathered pot.
But I've watched
The lives around me
Ascend from hollowest depths;
Souls that rise

To find their fill
And heroically live on
As stalwarts will.
I'll abide
My time of suffering
And though
Flesh may fade
And light be shadowed
Into darkest shade
My bright spot of spirit
Will triumphantly uncover
My victorious flame
That adversity flickered
Cannot be smothered.

GENERATIONS

See the contrast
of our hands, baby.
Your hands began a
short time ago
Formed in embryo,
Every finger a
root of the tree
Made perfectly
smooth and unweathered.
My hands, however,
have been together
for a long time now.
See how many lines
Wriggle amongst my flesh,
Roads of my years–
I've traveled a lot.
My handmap is made of
veinous mountains and
wrinkled valleys.
My fingers have many leaves
and many highways.
No, there's nothing of the road
on your hands yet.
So let me
hold your hand,
Now that you're on the outside
I'll be your guide
Until you can read
a map of your own.

And when you're grown
All your creasings will cradle
Your baby's unfolded flower
Just as my mother's map
Who has so many more lines,
Held mine.

THE MAKESHIFT MOTHER

The makeshift mother
Is built for bonds
And for breaking them
If they must
Be broken.
The makeshift mother
Makes temporary beds
Where temporary heads
Come to stay
When their other mother
Has thrown them away
Or was very terrible
At making beds herself.
The makeshift mother
Feeds, and fills plates
and stomachs to
Nourish those she
Only sees nourished
For their visit and then
That nourishment
Will go elsewhere,
According to State.
The makeshift mother
Takes one, takes two
Sometimes a sister
And a brother
Or more
If they can find
A makeshift mother
Who doesn't mind

And has the room
For the keeping
That often wants
To stay sleeping
Under one roof.
The makeshift mother
Tries to stay aloof,
Tries to be more
Of a hotel–
She has so many guests–
Children checking in and out
But gets to know
Them too well,
Tries to be welcoming
But not too warm
Tries to hold in her arms
Not too close,
Not to heart.
Tries to be as
Makeshift as possible.
The brief tenancies
Can be brutal,
But the makeshift mother
Makes love, gives home.
She gives whatever she has
For as long as it
Will be taken.
The makeshift mother
Is surrogate and shift.
The makeshift mother
Is a gift.

ON THE LAKE

He is rowing, rowing, rowing
Labored lengths in the going
But his arms ne'er slowing
The wooden boat.

It is floating, floating, floating
At the stillness shines a gloating
In pass and passenger it is toting
O'er the lake.

The water he is raking, raking, raking
With the oars smoothly making
A tiny tidal mergence waking
As he goes.

Alas, the day is closing, closing, closing!
Soon the sun sets for dozing
With the moon highly posing
In the sky.

He is trying, trying, trying
Stop the blaze from downward dying
The night to daytime prying
In his light.

Faster now for fighting, fighting, fighting
He serves strokes against the sighting
Brazen bolds insists on brighting–
This day will last!

To the lunar orb his will is blasting, blasting, blasting
To the sun his line is casting
Holding it to horizon, like floater fasting
It must not set!

He flings out his netting, netting, netting
Enmeshing captured moment wetting
Clock and time has lost its betting–
The night's no more.

In the blueness birds are soaring, soaring, soaring
Still he calmly continues oaring
He has forced perpetual morning
On the lake.

PERHAPS TO WoRK

Perhaps when we are older
We will meet
Again in our past fire
Tho' the years doused it drier
But not complete
As coals do smoulder.

Perhaps when I am gray
And my life has been lived
And I have fulfilled duty
Tho' sacrificed some beauty
A price I wanted to give
For the better way.

Perhaps then I will say
I did it all for you
And now I do what I wish for me
And follow a heart aged but free
To a love born deep and true
Rising now from where it lay.

Perhaps it will lead me back to you
After those many years
I do not know if it will
But as now younger
My appetite will hunger
As time may make it grow
Till I am old and starving through.

But perhaps the clock will advance
With no road for us to meet
Just lights in the heavens for us to gaze
And remember the sweet, bygone days
Still traveling separate on our street
Yet united at every upward glance,
Our hearts rejoined when starts do dance.

THE BALLAD OF BOBBY JOE

Oh, Bobby Joe, he did not know
That love is like the sea
For his boat riding on its flow
Cared not what color the vessels be.

But other beings, similarly sailing
Are marked as black or white
The flag flying may be railing
But the Captain is ever tight.

And Bobby Joe, he aimed his boat
Toward his lady love so true
But his Daddy came o'er to gloat
"Son, she's not the one for you–

Her hull is dark and small
Yours is light and fair
She has no sails at all
Her deck is barley and bare.

No, my son, it is not right
So keep your eyes out to sea
And look for a vessel that's pure and white
And knows its place, properly.

See your Mother's ship out there, my son–
She's anchored deep and true.
I knew, my boy, she was the one
With her gleaming eyes of blue.

Silly boy, your aim is hell!
You're not even headed toward a ship!
Excuse me, we raised you well–
Now conform to your supreme clip.

And sail away, away from her
Away from the pointed ebony!
Let me hear you say, 'Yes, sir!'
And then keep sailing next to me."

But Bobby Joe did not say
The things he was supposed to speak
His fancy boat was moving away,
The tidal tide was weak.

"Love has no color," said Bobby Joe,
"I'll abandon ship to prove to you
That I'll give up all for my lady's bow
And for love which is pure and true!

So, Daddy, take your money and your white
I do not care for it, or sadly, much for you."
And with that he left the wrong for the right
And stepped inside his lady love's canoe.

HUNTERS

The silver seagull swoops
Casting a staggered shadow
On the sharded mirror of waves
Pushed into scattered ridges–
His feathers, like a thousand fingers
Feel the air for grooves
To obtain floating,
Navigation niches
Yearning freedom and wings
Cozily outstretched into a
Yawning expansion–
Part of a parallel pursuing,
Stalking the slippery shimmy
Of a flightful fish
Targeted like a deer in the woods.

The seagull pursues a casual chase
A race of no intention
Shallower than the flirtations
Of a loyally married man,
He dives–
Of course, no catch.

A beholder might breathe
Disappointment;
Yet in a mind too small
To be credited cunning,
He obtains his original victory:

Enjoying, feeling, being,
Living fun-game freedom–

Like the hunter's
Half-marked silver shell
Falling harmlessly on the
Rusty sea of leaves
Lying languidly
In the forest.

HUNGERING

All the product, life's grand amalgamation
To the writing, the forming of this pen
Formed by swirling, creative fascination
Of One, made by many, contemplates again
The making of that which shaped her
And memories meet, intervene
With what could cause current pleasure
Instead life, lust and loss careen
And clash in a sort of torture
A constant disturbance of the mind.
Will peace sift for reveries pure
And a heart-calming confection find?
I fear that taste will not let her forget
And love go on hungering yet.

EXCUSED

Dumb how I miss you now that you're gone
Though it was I who excused you
Pardoned your presence rashly and wrong
Dumb how I miss you now that you're gone
Took the constant sweetness of your song
Flittered it byward, foolishly, too–
Dumb how I miss you now that you're gone
Though it was I who excused you.

THAT NIGHT IN THE HOUSE

I felt you once
Your skin
Wet and warm
The smoothness of your arm
In the hushed house
On the street
Where we did not live
My hand against
Your body sweet
And up to the back
Of your neck
Strengthening the pull
Hot and full
Drawing down your lips
Upon mine.

You said you admired
The perfect curve
Of my hips
Following the flow
With your fingertips
I let you linger,
I wanted to.
And I wanted
To stay in that
House forever

Whatever
Ended that night
I do not know

Although
We kissed in the dark
I cannot let
The brightness go.

CRAZY SUSAN AND THE SUN

She is waving to the redcoats
In rows upon the lawn
Firing cannonballed cookies
Chipping the sun
Opening wide his yellow mouth
And the ammunition is gone!
"Oh! Keep shooting skyward the wafers,"
Smiling Helios cries
Catching sweets instead of stars
With milk and saucer eyes.
Susan spinning round and round,
Round and round is she:
"But, dear!" she shouts into the blue,
"I'd rather hoped for tea!"
"Then bring new biscuits," Sun replies
"And pour a spot of tea
And we'll eat amongst the regiment,
Grand! Just you and me!"
Crazy Susan set the table
She spread the cloth so white
Then floated up to get her guest
Upon a stripe'd kite.
"Come down, dear, the cup's getting cold,
The table is laid and spread."
She offered her arm but
The sun gallant and gold
Offered her a ray instead.
The wind, gentle, obliged the date
Ceased every current and stirred

Made the kite plummet downward
Like a stricken, spiraling bird.
A breeze seated the sun;
Crazy Susan took a chair–
They sipped, then dined on almond toast
And fancy sugared pears.
The seating shone blinding bright!
But the rest o' the world was dark
For Susan had coaxed down the lamp
That lumined a global park.
"Oh! Dear!" Susan exclaimed
Noticing the blackness of the sky
Though scarcely noon
The stars still asleep
For the time for shining not soon.
"Drink your tea!" She insisted
"We must be fast to finish our cups!
Then shoot you faster than a star
And brighten the world back up!"
The sun was loath to hurry
For it had been such a long, long time
Since he vacationed properly
Or had biscuits so tasty and fine.
So he let the land wither
Till he held an empty plate
And sipped languidly
Till the hour was good and late.
Then Crazy Susan, surprised she saw
A faint glow up in the sky
And the Sun was smirking comfortably
A twinkle in his eye.

Slowly the world softly brightened,
A new day seemed to drift
Upward as the clock punched time
On the moon's punctual night shift.
"Do not fret, my dear," said Sun
"I have plenty of time now, you see.
So let's dine! Shall we invite the troops
To another cup of tea?"

RIVER DREAMS

It was in the morning
When I awoke
I knew it was a dream
Yet felt as wet
As if I'd swam
Through a real and rushing stream.
The memories my mind
Had made
Babbled back when in the night
They poured from within
My brain
They swelled and surged in sight
And a river of life
It played itself
Upon my sleeping screen
The banks were bursting
With the flood of it
The grass was lush and green
And in my bed
I sought to try
To remain unaffected,
Detached and dry–
I put on the current
The tightest clamp,
Yet every dawn
My sheets are damp.

FOR HIM

If part of me had tried
I might
Be lying in a different bed.
If some of me had sped
In reverse of flight
At first sight
Of feather wafting
Down dead
I might
Be resting next to you.
If the girl had known–
Wouldn't she wish she knew–
How the woman has grown
And so flown
Like a frantic mother bird
Fleeting back to the nest
Knowing one is falling
Prematurely and
Will die
But still must try her best?
'Tis little sense to some
To rush back home.
Yet she flies not to save
But weep softly at the grave.
And so I return my love to you
And mourn–
It's all I can do.

THE WINDOW

You came and opened my window
My breeze and breath began to blow
Out into the accepting air
Our past fixed frame and rigid flow

I floatingly followed you there
Outside, invisible and bare
You and the sun equally bright
I was a stranger to the glare

But I adjusted to the light
Released, you freed me into flight
Watch me dance! Listen to me sing!
With each current I swirled in sight

You're my second chance, other wing
Now in full view and everything
Reveals us both, yet just one ring
Encircling atmosphere of spring.

SLEEPING

You embrace
Me roundly
Encircling soundly
Figure and face
As the watchful white
Of an ethereal egg
Crossed-over leg
And amorous arm
Enfolded neatly
Body blanket
Covering completely
Sigh like satin sweetly
Enveloping, enshrouded
All nucleus night
Till the morning
Cellular and light
Clammed and closed
And unclouded
A love repose
Zipped up tightly
In lining
Restful reclining
Backward into you
And into bliss
And you kiss
Me with our nestful need
Having built yourself
In loving layers
All around me

In warmth and
Whispered wizardry
For my succulent keeping
And hold me
Having a haven
While I'm sleeping.

OUR SEA

Oh, my dear,
How you bright me
Light me
Every fire ignite me
Flashing flesh and fervor
Moan and murmur
A red rush
Your lips lush
Making my body blush
We pulse and please
Heat increase
Fuel the fevered flush
To the glorious gush
Your touch to thrill
And I spill
Over to ecstasy
You and me
Our whole selves free
Give more and more and more
Rocket shot
To ceiling from floor
Bonds and blending
Every nerve expending
Electric integration
Cosmic sensation
But is beauty beyond
It's an underlying quake
Beneath the orgasmic ocean
The swelling tides of motion

Our souls make
So much more
Than watery waves
A seismic emotion
Coursing deeper than
Surface satisfaction
You reach and rock
Me from
The rippling top
To the depths
So down below
Only you know
And only you touch
And only you cause and keep
The secret completion
Of me, from the
Very ocean deep
To the top tips
Of the sea.

UPLIFTED

All alone am I dying
Hear my soul softly crying
As my sorrows go a-flying
In the night.

Riding heavy on the faintest beam of light
Rays carry the echo of my voice to freedom's land
Where without my thoughts of drowning
And a countenance of frowning
They are given choice of bounding
Past my hand

That has held them captive in a spirit-saddened state.
But freed by heaven's intervention
They crack-split chains of forced constriction
Now directing a glad convention
'Round my gate.

Jubilantly free of degradation
Tones rise from belated separation
To discover glee with fascination
It was forgot.

And rallying with an optimistic plot,
I am surrounded by their newly upturned faces
That clamor chords of old beginnings
Before life sheared uneven thinnings
When only grew delightful winnings
And candied graces.

And their smiles remind me
Of the smiles that used to be
And despite my pity pooling
Puddles of sorrow that were grueling
Have dried up their fretful fooling
Releasing me.

And now I soar with the
Echoes of my voice
That by changing the original
Course of their state
Have given me new cause for singing
A lighter spirit happily ringing
And left to fly as birds winging
Without weight.